COSMIC HEMP PATHWAYS

COSMIC HEMP PATHWAYS

MATTHEW PETCHINSKY

Apophis Enterprises LLC

CHAPTER 1

<u>Cosmic Hemp Pathways</u>
By: Matthew Petchinsky

Introduction: Unveiling the Mystical Alliance of Hemp and Astrology

Overview: Presenting the Unique Interplay

In an age where holistic wellness and spiritual exploration are increasingly sought after, a captivating interplay emerges between two ancient, potent forces: hemp and astrology. Hemp, a resilient plant deeply rooted in history, holds multifaceted benefits ranging from medicinal to spiritual. Meanwhile, astrology—the ancient practice of understanding cosmic patterns—offers insights into the timing and nature of our lives. Together, these potent traditions form a unique synergy. This book, *Cosmic Hemp Pathways*, unveils this mystical alliance, exploring how hemp's versatile qualities and astrological cycles work harmoniously to facilitate healing, personal transformation, and spiritual enlightenment.

As we delve into the layers of this mystical relationship, we'll uncover how hemp's distinct properties align with astrological forces to amplify its benefits. From enhancing meditation practices to synchronizing with the lunar phases, we will illuminate how hemp's use—whether through tinctures, infusions, or ritualistic applications—is enriched by astrological wisdom. Ultimately, this book seeks to guide readers on how to weave these two profound traditions into their daily lives for greater personal fulfillment.

Purpose: Exploring Cosmic Connections

The purpose of *Cosmic Hemp Pathways* is to uncover the cosmic connections that empower hemp's use. Through examining the astrological cycles and their impact on human life, we aim to illustrate how certain celestial events can amplify or attenuate the effects of hemp. By understanding the planetary alignments, lunar phases, and astrological signs, readers will learn how to harness the plant's properties to align with their unique energetic blueprint. This book strives to deepen your understanding of the cosmic interplay that shapes our realities, providing tools to maximize hemp's medicinal and spiritual effects.

We will explore how hemp serves as a conduit for spiritual connection, helping individuals tap into higher states of consciousness. You will find practical tips for integrating hemp into your personal rituals and uncover ways to synchronize its use with the rhythms of the cosmos. By learning to align hemp's applications with favorable astrological cycles, you can enhance your well-being and spiritual growth.

Foundation: Understanding Hemp and Astrology

Before embarking on this journey through the cosmic hemp pathways, it is vital to establish a solid understanding of both hemp and astrology.

- **Hemp**: With its storied history, hemp has been cultivated and used for various purposes across cultures and millennia. This versatile plant can be processed into textiles, oils, and medicinal products. Its non-psychoactive nature makes it a potent aid in reducing anxiety, managing pain, and promoting relaxation. Key types include industrial hemp for fibers and seeds, and cannabidiol (CBD) varieties for medicinal extracts. We'll delve into how cultivation practices, processing methods, and usage traditions shape its properties and applications.

- **Astrology**: As one of humanity's oldest systems of understanding the cosmos, astrology deciphers the patterns and movements of celestial bodies to offer insights into personality, timing, and purpose. Key principles include the zodiac signs, lunar phases, planetary aspects, and transits. This foundation will serve as a compass for aligning hemp's use with astrological forces. We will explain the influence of each sign on the body, mind, and spirit, and provide an overview of planetary cycles crucial to interpreting timing and energies.

With these foundational principles, readers will be well-equipped to explore the fascinating realm where hemp and astrology intersect. Through the pages of *Cosmic Hemp Pathways*, you will discover practical guidance on integrating these practices for deeper healing, spiritual growth, and personal empowerment.

Check out my Virtual dispensary for all your hemp needs: https://shift.store/sg1fan23477/retail

Chapter 1: Historical and Cultural Journey of Hemp
Ancient Times: Hemp's Origins and Historical Uses

In tracing the lineage of hemp across millennia, we unearth a fascinating journey rooted in tradition, medicine, and ritual. Hemp's origins can be traced back to ancient regions like East Asia and the Mediterranean, where it was cherished for its versatility. Archaeological evidence reveals that hemp cultivation dates back over 10,000 years, making it one of humanity's earliest domesticated plants.

1. **Asia:** In ancient China, hemp, known as "ma," played a vital role in traditional medicine, textiles, and spiritual practices. The Chinese used hemp to produce fiber for textiles and paper as early as 2800 BCE, and its medicinal properties were recorded in the *Shen Nong Ben Cao Jing*—a classical text attributed to the mythical Chinese emperor Shen Nong. Here, it was lauded for its ability to relieve pain, treat gout, and aid digestive health. It also found ritualistic use in offerings to gods and as part of ceremonial rites.

2. **India:** In India, hemp emerged as "bhang" or "ganja," an integral part of Ayurvedic medicine and religious customs. In the Vedic texts, cannabis was considered a sacred plant with divine associations. Devotees used it to deepen meditation, connect with Shiva (the god of destruction and transformation), and to achieve higher states of consciousness during religious festivals. Ayurvedic texts highlight its uses in alleviating insomnia, anxiety, and digestive ailments.

3. **Middle East and Mediterranean:** Across ancient Egypt, Persia, and Greece, hemp was embraced for its medicinal, textile, and psychoactive properties. Egyptian healers applied hemp as a poultice for sore eyes and inflamed skin. In Persia, it was valued in religious rites and healing. The Greek historian Herodotus chronicled its recreational and therapeutic uses among the Scythians, who used hemp fumes to achieve trance-like states.

4. **Europe**: In medieval Europe, hemp gained prominence for its fibrous strength and medicinal properties. Monks grew hemp in monastery gardens to produce ropes, sacks, and healing balms. Medieval apothecaries often prescribed hemp to soothe pain, treat seizures, and aid in childbirth. By the Renaissance, hemp had spread throughout Europe as a critical crop in medicine and textiles.

Modern Resurgence: Contemporary Revival of Hemp

Despite its long-standing historical use, hemp's prominence waned during the 20th century due to legal restrictions, changing cultural perceptions, and the rise of synthetic fibers. The passage of prohibitive laws criminalized cannabis in many regions, overshadowing hemp's practical and spiritual legacy. However, in recent decades, global recognition of its therapeutic potential has reignited interest.

1. **Holistic and Alternative Therapies**: The contemporary revival of hemp is partly fueled by a resurgence in holistic and alternative medicine. With CBD extracts emerging as potent remedies for inflammation, anxiety, and chronic pain, a new generation of health practitioners, patients, and advocates are exploring its therapeutic spectrum. Hemp's anti-inflammatory and neuroprotective properties are being researched to address a host of ailments, while its naturally relaxing effects make it a preferred supplement for meditation, yoga, and mindfulness practices.

2. **Legal Landscape**: Changing legislation around the world has gradually opened doors to hemp cultivation and usage. Many countries and U.S. states have legalized or decriminalized hemp-based products, recognizing the economic, medicinal, and environmental potential. This legislative shift is driving innovation in hemp-based textiles, bioplastics, and building materials, offering sustainable alternatives to traditional resources.

3. **Cultural Reawakening**: Alongside legalization, a cultural reawakening to hemp's spiritual roots is taking shape. Its role

in sacred rituals and traditional healing is being revisited and adapted to modern spiritual practices. Individuals are incorporating hemp in their spiritual journeys for its ability to heighten awareness and facilitate deep meditation. Moreover, the renewed emphasis on sustainability aligns with hemp's environmental benefits, making it a symbol of holistic living.

Cosmic Hemp Pathways invites readers to recognize the historical and cultural richness of hemp. From ancient civilizations to contemporary revivals, this plant's journey reveals an evolving narrative of healing, spirituality, and transformation that transcends time and borders. As we continue in the book, we'll explore how aligning hemp's versatile benefits with cosmic cycles can create a harmonious path toward personal fulfillment.

Check out my Virtual dispensary for all your hemp needs: https://shift.store/sg1fan23477/retail

Chapter 2: Astrological Foundations Relevant to Herbalism
Astrological Basics: Key Concepts of Astrology

Astrology provides a framework for understanding the universe's cosmic forces, decoding the celestial patterns that shape our lives. To weave astrological insights into herbalism, we must establish a strong foundational understanding of the essential concepts:

1. **Zodiac Signs**: The zodiac consists of twelve signs, each representing unique characteristics influenced by elemental energies (fire, earth, air, and water). They are divided into cardinal, fixed, and mutable modalities based on how their energies manifest. The signs are:
   - **Aries** (Fire, Cardinal): Bold, pioneering, and action-oriented.
   - **Taurus** (Earth, Fixed): Sensual, grounded, and patient.
   - **Gemini** (Air, Mutable): Curious, communicative, and adaptable.
   - **Cancer** (Water, Cardinal): Nurturing, intuitive, and protective.
   - **Leo** (Fire, Fixed): Creative, confident, and generous.
   - **Virgo** (Earth, Mutable): Analytical, meticulous, and health-conscious.
   - **Libra** (Air, Cardinal): Harmonious, diplomatic, and aesthetic-minded.
   - **Scorpio** (Water, Fixed): Passionate, intense, and transformative.
   - **Sagittarius** (Fire, Mutable): Adventurous, philosophical, and optimistic.
   - **Capricorn** (Earth, Cardinal): Disciplined, ambitious, and responsible.
   - **Aquarius** (Air, Fixed): Innovative, independent, and humanitarian.

- **Pisces** (Water, Mutable): Compassionate, imaginative, and empathetic.

2. **Planets and Their Influences**: The planets serve as energetic symbols influencing personality, emotions, and behavior. In herbalism, planetary energies are often linked with specific plants that embody their qualities:
   - **Sun**: The core self, vitality, and creativity.
   - **Moon**: Emotions, instincts, and intuition.
   - **Mercury**: Communication, intellect, and adaptability.
   - **Venus**: Love, beauty, and harmony.
   - **Mars**: Action, desire, and assertiveness.
   - **Jupiter**: Expansion, wisdom, and optimism.
   - **Saturn**: Discipline, structure, and perseverance.
   - **Uranus**: Innovation, rebellion, and sudden changes.
   - **Neptune**: Dreams, spirituality, and illusions.
   - **Pluto**: Transformation, power, and rebirth.

3. **Celestial Cycles**: Celestial cycles reflect the rhythm of time and life processes. They include:
   - **Solar Cycle**: The Sun moves through the zodiac annually, influencing each season and sign's energies.
   - **Lunar Cycle**: The Moon's phases (new, first quarter, full, last quarter) influence emotional tides and intuition, providing a rhythm for growth, manifestation, and release.
   - **Planetary Retrogrades**: When a planet appears to move backward, its influence intensifies, often bringing reflection and reassessment.
   - **Planetary Transits**: The planets' movements through the signs highlight favorable or challenging periods for various activities.

Link to Herbalism: Celestial Influences on Plant-Based Healing
Astrological principles enrich the field of herbalism by revealing how celestial cycles and planetary alignments shape plant growth, potency,

and efficacy. By understanding these correlations, herbalists can maximize the healing potential of plants like hemp.

1. **Planetary Correspondences**: In traditional herbalism, plants are associated with planetary energies based on their appearance, effects, and medicinal properties.
   - **Sun**: Plants ruled by the Sun (e.g., St. John's Wort) have warming, invigorating effects, promoting vitality.
   - **Moon**: Lunar plants (e.g., chamomile) support emotional balance and relaxation.
   - **Mercury**: Mercurial herbs (e.g., lavender) enhance communication and mental clarity.
   - **Venus**: Venus-ruled plants (e.g., rose) promote love, beauty, and harmony.
   - **Mars**: Martial plants (e.g., cayenne pepper) stimulate circulation and boost energy.
   - **Jupiter**: Jovian herbs (e.g., dandelion) are expansive, promoting growth and abundance.
   - **Saturn**: Saturnian plants (e.g., comfrey) aid structure and endurance, often strengthening bones or joints.

2. **Celestial Cycles and Plant Growth**: Astrological cycles offer guidelines for cultivating, harvesting, and using plants for maximum potency:
   - **Lunar Phases**: Each lunar phase influences plant development:
     - New Moon: Ideal for sowing seeds and planting crops that thrive below ground.
     - First Quarter: A time for transplanting and nurturing above-ground crops.
     - Full Moon: A peak period for harvesting, when plants are at their most potent.
     - Last Quarter: Suitable for pruning and weeding.
   - **Planetary Transits**: When the planets transit favorable signs for certain plants, it may enhance their growth or

healing effects. For instance, harvesting calming herbs during a Moon transit through Cancer or Pisces can enhance their soothing qualities.

- **Zodiac Signs**: Each zodiac sign imparts specific energies influencing plant care:
  - Fertile signs (Cancer, Scorpio, Pisces) are best for planting and nurturing.
  - Barren signs (Aries, Leo, Sagittarius) are more suitable for pruning and weeding.

3. **Astrological Timing for Herbal Remedies**: Aligning herbal use with celestial events can amplify their efficacy. For example:
   - Taking tinctures during lunar phases linked to cleansing can deepen detoxification.
   - Applying salves under specific planetary transits may accelerate healing in targeted areas.

Cosmic Hemp Pathways will guide readers through harnessing these astrological principles in herbalism. By aligning plant-based practices with cosmic cycles, readers can create a holistic path to wellness that leverages the mystical alliance between plants and the stars.

Check out my Virtual dispensary for all your hemp needs: https://shift.store/sg1fan23477/retail

Chapter 3: Hemp and the Sun - Vitality and Life Force
Solar Connection: How the Sun Influences Hemp's Qualities
The Sun, symbolizing vitality, life force, and growth, holds a unique relationship with all plants, but its influence on hemp is especially noteworthy. As the source of light and warmth, the Sun plays a pivotal role in shaping hemp's growth, potency, and energetic properties.

1. **Life-Giving Energy**: The Sun governs the energy of growth and renewal. In hemp, this translates to robust development of cannabinoids like cannabidiol (CBD), terpenes, and essential oils that define the plant's distinctive qualities. These compounds exhibit invigorating, protective, and revitalizing effects—mirroring the Sun's life-sustaining energy.

2. **Zodiac and Solar Influences**: The Sun's journey through the zodiac signs brings varying energetic influences that can affect hemp's growth and potency:
    - **Aries (March 21 - April 19)**: As a fire sign, Aries stimulates rapid growth and promotes vitality. Hemp grown or harvested under Aries can embody the boldness and pioneering spirit of the sign.
    - **Taurus (April 20 - May 20)**: As an earth sign ruled by Venus, Taurus fosters stability and steady growth. Hemp harvested during this period is often more aromatic and deeply calming.
    - **Leo (July 23 - August 22)**: Leo's solar rulership magnifies the Sun's influence, enhancing creativity, expression, and strength in hemp's properties.
    - **Sagittarius (November 22 - December 21)**: Another fire sign, Sagittarius embodies optimism and expansion. Hemp grown or harvested during this time can exhibit properties that support mental clarity and higher purpose.

3. **Solar Seasons**: The Sun's transit through the four seasons influences hemp's overall health and growth cycle:
    ◦ **Spring**: The vernal equinox marks the Sun's entry into Aries, signaling renewal and growth. Hemp sown in spring flourishes under the strengthening sunlight, developing its essential compounds and oils.
    ◦ **Summer**: As the Sun reaches its zenith during the summer solstice, hemp plants benefit from maximum daylight and warmth, accelerating flowering and cannabinoid synthesis.
    ◦ **Autumn**: During the autumnal equinox, the waning daylight prompts hemp to enter its final stages of flowering and resin production, ensuring peak potency.
    ◦ **Winter**: Although winter marks a period of dormancy for most plants, hemp preparations such as tinctures and oils can be produced and stored for their warming and revitalizing properties.

Practical Applications: Cultivating and Harvesting Hemp by Solar Phases

Understanding the interplay between the Sun and hemp allows cultivators to harness solar energy for optimum potency.

1. **Cultivation**:
    ◦ **Seed Sowing**: The best times to sow hemp seeds coincide with the spring and early summer months, as the Sun climbs in strength. During these solar phases, warmth and daylight support robust germination.
    ◦ **Transplanting**: For outdoor cultivation, transplanting should occur once the seedlings are sturdy and the spring frost has passed. The lengthening daylight hours promote strong root establishment and vegetative growth.
2. **Harvesting**:
    ◦ **Full Bloom**: Hemp's flowering phase is influenced by the solar light cycle. In the northern hemisphere, harvesting

typically begins in late summer and continues through autumn, depending on the variety. Harvesting during the high solar months of August and September ensures peak resin production.

- ◦ **Solar Day Timing**: Harvesting early in the morning, just after sunrise, allows the flowers and leaves to retain their essential oils and cannabinoids due to the cooler temperatures.

3. **Post-Harvest Processing**:
    - ◦ **Drying and Curing**: After harvesting, hemp should be dried in a shaded, well-ventilated area. Avoid direct sunlight, as excessive heat can degrade the plant's vital compounds. Proper curing during this period ensures the preservation of potency.
    - ◦ **Storage**: Once cured, hemp preparations should be stored in opaque, airtight containers away from direct sunlight to maintain their energetic properties.

4. **Seasonal Preparations**:
    - ◦ **Spring and Summer Tinctures**: Solar tinctures prepared during spring and summer embody vitality and vigor. These tinctures can be charged under direct sunlight to imbue them with additional solar energy.
    - ◦ **Autumn and Winter Oils**: In colder months, warming hemp-infused oils are useful for soothing muscle aches and boosting circulation. They can be enhanced by infusing them with solar-charged herbs like St. John's Wort.

Cosmic Hemp Pathways encourages readers to integrate solar wisdom into their hemp practices, recognizing the Sun's unique role in bringing vitality and life force. By aligning hemp's cultivation and harvesting cycles with the Sun's energy, practitioners can achieve a holistic balance that enriches the plant's natural benefits.

Check out my Virtual dispensary for all your hemp needs: https://shift.store/sg1fan23477/retail

Chapter 4: Hemp and the Moon - Intuition and Emotional Healing

Lunar Phases: The Moon's Influence on Hemp Cultivation and Usage

The Moon governs the subtle realms of emotion, intuition, and spiritual energy. Its phases profoundly affect the growth and potency of plants like hemp, which thrive in resonance with the lunar rhythm. As the Moon waxes and wanes, it offers insights into how to cultivate and use hemp for emotional balance, spiritual practices, and intuitive guidance.

1. **New Moon**: The New Moon is a time of introspection and renewal. The dark sky marks a metaphorical blank slate, making it ideal for setting intentions and planting seeds—both literally and figuratively.

    ◦ **Cultivation**: Seeds sown at this time benefit from the strong upward energy that follows during the waxing phase. New growth in hemp plants is nurtured by this phase, resulting in vigorous root development.

    ◦ **Usage**: During the New Moon, hemp can be used to initiate emotional healing and set intentions. This is an ideal phase for consuming hemp-based tinctures and teas to calm the mind and focus on new beginnings.

2. **Waxing Crescent to First Quarter**: As the Moon shifts from the slender crescent to the first quarter, energy builds, fostering gradual growth and forward movement.

    ◦ **Cultivation**: This is a favorable time to transplant hemp seedlings. As the Moon's energy increases, it supports healthy leaf and stalk development.

    ◦ **Usage**: Hemp-infused oils or topical salves can be applied to support strength and vitality. Consuming hemp in these phases can boost motivation and creativity.

3. **Waxing Gibbous to Full Moon**: The Full Moon is the peak of lunar energy, symbolizing culmination, manifestation, and heightened emotions.
    ◦ **Cultivation**: Hemp plants absorb the Moon's maximum gravitational pull during this time, promoting resin production. This phase is ideal for harvesting flowers and leaves at peak potency.
    ◦ **Usage**: Full Moon rituals benefit from hemp's amplifying effects on intuition and spirituality. Meditative practices involving hemp can reach deeper states, helping to release emotional blockages. This is a powerful time to work with hemp tinctures or vaporizers for introspective healing.
4. **Waning Gibbous to Last Quarter**: The waning period symbolizes release and surrender as the Moon transitions from gibbous to the third quarter.
    ◦ **Cultivation**: This phase supports pruning and clearing away unnecessary plant material, redirecting energy toward essential growth.
    ◦ **Usage**: Hemp consumption can facilitate emotional detoxification during this period. Making space in the mind and heart through hemp-based meditation allows suppressed emotions to surface and heal.
5. **Waning Crescent**: The final lunar phase before the New Moon is a reflective time, preparing for the new cycle ahead.
    ◦ **Cultivation**: This period is best for soil preparation and composting, ensuring a fertile foundation for the next cycle of growth.
    ◦ **Usage**: Hemp applications during the waning crescent are calming and grounding. Infusing hemp oils with other soothing herbs like lavender or chamomile enhances their relaxing qualities.

Usage Tips: Integrating Hemp into Lunar Phases for Healing

Harnessing lunar energy enhances the potency and impact of hemp in spiritual and emotional practices. Here are tips for using hemp during different phases:

1. **New Moon:**
   - Set intentions for emotional healing while drinking hemp-infused tea.
   - Incorporate hemp flower smoke or vapor into rituals to clear mental clutter.

2. **Waxing Crescent to First Quarter:**
   - Apply hemp-infused topical oils to stimulate creativity and action.
   - Create an altar with hemp flowers and crystals to foster strength and new growth.

3. **Waxing Gibbous to Full Moon:**
   - Meditate with hemp tinctures to access intuitive insights.
   - Hold a ceremony to manifest your deepest emotional desires using hemp resin.

4. **Waning Gibbous to Last Quarter:**
   - Perform a cleansing ritual by smudging with hemp smoke to release negative energies.
   - Incorporate hemp essential oils in diffusers to support inner clarity.

5. **Waning Crescent:**
   - Engage in deep meditation with hemp-infused candles or oils.
   - Journal about emotional healing progress while consuming hemp-infused tea.

Cosmic Hemp Pathways encourages readers to align hemp use with the Moon's powerful rhythms. This harmonious integration amplifies the plant's ability to heal emotions, heighten intuition, and guide spiritual journeys toward deeper fulfillment.

Check out my Virtual dispensary for all your hemp needs: https://shift.store/sg1fan23477/retail

Chapter 5: Mercury and Hemp - Communication and Cognition
Mercurial Influence: How Mercury Affects Hemp's Role in Communication and Cognition

In astrology, Mercury rules communication, intellect, and mental agility, directly influencing how we perceive and express ideas. The planet embodies adaptability, analysis, and swiftness, which directly correlate with the qualities of hemp as a mental and communicative enhancer. Hemp's natural compounds, including cannabinoids and terpenes, help unlock these cognitive faculties, providing clarity and ease in communication. Understanding Mercury's cycles can help us harness hemp's properties effectively.

1. **Cognitive Stimulation**: Hemp's compounds, particularly cannabidiol (CBD), interact with our endocannabinoid system to promote mental balance. These effects can align with Mercury's analytical energy to sharpen focus and improve memory.
2. **Expression and Creativity**: Mercury inspires creativity and verbal eloquence. Hemp's relaxing yet stimulating effects help overcome communication barriers, fostering clearer self-expression and imaginative thinking.
3. **Adaptability**: Mercury's influence promotes flexibility and problem-solving skills. Hemp supports this adaptability by reducing mental stress and encouraging open-mindedness.
4. **Mercurial Cycles**: The three-week cycles of Mercury Retrograde occur several times annually, often accompanied by communication breakdowns, misunderstandings, and delays. Hemp can alleviate these effects by grounding and centering the mind. Mercury also exhibits greater influence in specific zodiac signs, amplifying its impact on cognition:
   - **Gemini**: Mercury is most comfortable in Gemini, its ruling sign, enhancing curiosity and intellectual exploration. Hemp can help expand on Gemini's inquisitiveness.

- ° **Virgo**: In Virgo, Mercury promotes organization and precision, skills that hemp can support by reducing distractions and improving concentration.

Recommendations: Using Hemp to Enhance Communication Skills and Mental Clarity

To effectively harness the combined energies of hemp and Mercury, one should consider different methods that align with the planet's phases and influence:

1. **Daily Rituals for Cognitive Clarity**:
   - ° **Tinctures and Capsules**: Incorporate hemp-based tinctures or capsules in morning or afternoon routines to support mental clarity throughout the day.
   - ° **Topicals**: Apply hemp-infused oils or balms to temples or neck before studying, writing, or brainstorming sessions.
2. **Communication Techniques**:
   - ° **Teas and Infusions**: Use hemp tea blends to calm nerves before giving a speech, presentation, or important conversation.
   - ° **Aromatherapy**: Inhale hemp essential oils through diffusers or inhalers to stimulate focus and clear expression.
3. **Adaptability During Mercury Retrograde**:
   - ° **Vaping or Smoking**: Consider hemp flower vapor or smoke to rapidly calm the mind and ground oneself during challenging conversations.
   - ° **Journaling**: Write down thoughts while using hemp tinctures or edibles to reflect on communication issues that arise, especially during retrograde periods.
4. **Harnessing Mercury in Specific Signs**:
   - ° **Gemini**: When Mercury transits Gemini, explore creative pursuits and networking opportunities. Pair social events with hemp teas to stay grounded while engaging others.

- **Virgo**: During Virgo transits, focus on problem-solving and organization. Try micro-dosing hemp-infused capsules to support task completion and productivity.

Cosmic Hemp Pathways guides readers through this intricate relationship between Mercury and hemp. By using hemp strategically to align with Mercury's influence, readers can bolster their communication skills and mental clarity while embracing adaptability. This synergy offers a holistic path for personal growth and success in both intellectual and expressive pursuits.

Check out my Virtual dispensary for all your hemp needs: https://shift.store/sg1fan23477/retail

Chapter 6: Venus and Hemp - Harmony and Relationships

Venusian Aspects: The Influence of Venus on Hemp and Relationships
Venus, the planet of love, beauty, and harmony, brings joy and balance into relationships. It symbolizes pleasure, attraction, and aesthetic appreciation, all of which resonate deeply with the qualities of hemp. By understanding the link between Venus and hemp, we can cultivate a harmonious blend that amplifies our ability to love, appreciate beauty, and nurture meaningful relationships.

1. **Love and Attraction**: Venus enhances our ability to attract and connect deeply with others, whether romantically or platonically. Hemp, with its calming effects and soothing qualities, helps us overcome stress and anxiety, enabling us to be fully present in our interactions.

2. **Beauty and Self-Care**: Venus also rules over beauty and aesthetics. Hemp's therapeutic compounds are known for nourishing the skin, enhancing radiance, and promoting relaxation. By integrating hemp into beauty routines, we can embody the Venusian principles of elegance and well-being.

3. **Interpersonal Harmony**: Relationships thrive under Venusian influence, as it encourages compassion and understanding. Hemp's mood-balancing properties can improve emotional regulation, helping to navigate conflicts with grace and empathy.

4. **Venusian Cycles**: The cycles of Venus affect how its energies manifest in our lives, impacting relationships and our personal sense of beauty.

    ○ **Retrograde**: When Venus is retrograde (every 18-19 months for about 40 days), it's a time to reassess relationships and self-worth. Hemp can be especially beneficial during this period, easing emotional discomfort and encouraging self-reflection.

- **Transits**: As Venus transits each zodiac sign, it shapes how we experience love, beauty, and harmony:
    - **Taurus and Libra** (Venus' ruling signs): Foster stability and fairness in relationships.
    - **Pisces**: Enhances sensitivity and emotional depth.
    - **Leo**: Boosts creative self-expression and passionate connections.

Hemp Recipes: Creating Products to Amplify Attraction and Emotional Connection

By using hemp strategically with Venusian principles, one can create products that promote personal attractiveness and strengthen emotional bonds.

1. **Hemp-Infused Bath Soak**:
    - **Ingredients**: Epsom salts, dried rose petals, hemp essential oil, lavender essential oil, Himalayan pink salt.
    - **Instructions**:
        1. Combine 1 cup Epsom salts, 1 tablespoon dried rose petals, and ½ cup Himalayan pink salt.
        2. Add 10 drops each of hemp and lavender essential oils.
        3. Stir well, store in a glass jar, and use a handful in warm bathwater to promote relaxation, rejuvenation, and heart-opening.
2. **Hemp and Rose Face Mask**:
    - **Ingredients**: Hemp oil, rose water, French pink clay, honey.
    - **Instructions**:
        1. Mix 2 tablespoons French pink clay, 1 tablespoon honey, and 1 teaspoon hemp oil.
        2. Add enough rose water to create a thick paste.
        3. Apply to the face for 10-15 minutes before rinsing off to rejuvenate the skin and imbue a radiant glow.
3. **Hemp Chocolates for Connection**:

- ◦ **Ingredients**: Hemp seeds, dark chocolate, sea salt, vanilla extract.
- ◦ **Instructions**:
  1. Melt 1 cup dark chocolate in a double boiler.
  2. Stir in ¼ cup hemp seeds, ½ teaspoon sea salt, and ½ teaspoon vanilla extract.
  3. Pour the mixture into molds or a baking sheet, and chill until set.
  4. Share these chocolates with a loved one to enhance shared affection.

4. **Hemp-Infused Massage Oil**:
   - ◦ **Ingredients**: Hemp oil, sweet almond oil, sandalwood essential oil, ylang-ylang essential oil.
   - ◦ **Instructions**:
     1. Mix 2 tablespoons hemp oil with 2 tablespoons sweet almond oil.
     2. Add 10 drops of sandalwood essential oil and 10 drops of ylang-ylang essential oil.
     3. Use this blend for gentle massages that promote intimacy and emotional relaxation.

Cosmic Hemp Pathways teaches readers how to blend Venusian energies with hemp to enrich relationships and personal beauty. By using these recipes thoughtfully, readers can create rituals that celebrate love, harmony, and self-care, fostering deep emotional connections.

Check out my Virtual dispensary for all your hemp needs: https://shift.store/sg1fan23477/retail

Chapter 7: Mars and Hemp - Energy and Assertion

Mars Alignment: How Mars Influences Hemp's Energy and Assertion

Mars, the planet of energy, drive, and assertion, rules over passion, ambition, and the will to overcome obstacles. Known as the god of war in Roman mythology, Mars inspires us to face challenges with courage and conviction. Hemp's diverse properties can complement these qualities by enhancing energy, sharpening focus, and reducing stress. Understanding how to harness hemp's properties with Mars' influence allows for a strategic approach to cultivating productivity, athleticism, and resilience.

1. **Physical Vitality**: Mars governs physical strength and endurance, traits that are vital for athletic and assertive pursuits. Hemp's cannabinoids, particularly CBD, interact with our endocannabinoid system to promote muscle relaxation, reduce inflammation, and aid recovery.

2. **Mental Focus and Determination**: Mars encourages focus and unwavering determination. Hemp's calming yet clarifying effects can sharpen concentration and help channel Mars' assertiveness toward positive, goal-oriented action.

3. **Overcoming Challenges**: Mars provides the inner strength to confront and navigate obstacles. Hemp reduces mental fatigue and stress, improving the resilience needed to manage and respond effectively to adversity.

4. **Mars Transits**: The alignment of Mars with zodiac signs and its retrograde cycles influence its expression.

- **Aries**: Mars rules Aries, where its energy is fiery, bold, and driven. Hemp can help manage impulsiveness while enhancing productivity and assertiveness.
- **Scorpio**: Mars also governs Scorpio, where its energy is intense and strategic. Hemp can balance this deep intensity with calming effects that bring clarity and emotional resilience.
- **Retrograde**: Mars retrograde (approximately every two years for about two months) can lead to frustration and stagnation. Hemp can soothe anxiety and impatience during these periods.

Guidance: Using Hemp to Boost Energy and Overcome Challenges

To harness Mars' energetic influence, consider incorporating hemp in strategic ways to improve physical vitality, resilience, and assertiveness.

1. **Pre-Workout Energizer**:
   - **Hemp-Infused Protein Shake**:
     - Mix 1 cup plant-based milk, 2 tablespoons hemp protein powder, 1 tablespoon nut butter, and 1 teaspoon honey.
     - Blend with ice for a nutrient-dense shake that provides energy, protein, and essential fatty acids to fuel physical activities.
2. **Post-Workout Recovery**:
   - **Hemp Bath Soak**:
     - Mix 1 cup Epsom salts, 2 tablespoons dried ginger powder, and 2 tablespoons hemp essential oil.
     - Add to warm bathwater for a soothing soak that eases sore muscles and reduces inflammation.
3. **Focus and Assertiveness Boost**:
   - **Hemp Tincture**:

- Take a micro-dose of hemp tincture in the morning before engaging in challenging tasks. The tincture can help improve focus, determination, and clarity.

4. **Mental Resilience:**
   - **Hemp-Infused Tea Blend:**
     - Combine dried hemp leaves with adaptogenic herbs like ashwagandha, lemon balm, and holy basil.
     - Brew into a calming tea that promotes mental resilience and reduces anxiety during times of high pressure.

5. **Mars Retrograde Strategies:**
   - **Meditative Rituals:**
     - Create a calming space with candles, crystals, and hemp essential oil diffusers.
     - Incorporate hemp-infused oils into breathing exercises to soothe agitation and improve adaptability.

Cosmic Hemp Pathways provides readers with a guide to unlocking Mars' power through hemp. By aligning the planet's energy with hemp's natural benefits, individuals can cultivate physical and mental endurance, overcome challenges, and embody a productive, assertive mindset.

Check out my Virtual dispensary for all your hemp needs: https://shift.store/sg1fan23477/retail

Chapter 8: Jupiter and Hemp - Growth and Prosperity

Jovian Promises: The Expansive Nature of Jupiter and Its Effect on Hemp Growth

Jupiter, the planet associated with expansion, abundance, and wisdom, exudes a benevolent energy that encourages growth and prosperity in all facets of life. Its influence is magnified in how hemp thrives and is utilized. Known as the "greater benefic," Jupiter's positive energies foster a broadening of horizons and support the flourishing of one's endeavors. By understanding the interplay between Jupiter's cycles and hemp's properties, we can amplify the plant's potential for healing and attracting prosperity.

1. **Growth and Vitality**: Jupiter's expansive energy encourages the rapid growth of plants, helping hemp flourish when the planet is prominent. The nutrient-rich compounds in hemp, particularly its essential fatty acids and proteins, symbolize this vitality.

2. **Abundance and Opportunity**: Jupiter inspires generosity and abundance, which can be harnessed through the cultivation and use of hemp products. Hemp is resilient, versatile, and sustainable, traits that align with Jupiter's ability to multiply opportunities.

3. **Wisdom and Spiritual Expansion**: Jupiter represents philosophical growth and spiritual exploration. Hemp's calming effects can elevate mindfulness practices, supporting deeper meditation, exploration of higher knowledge, and personal development.

4. **Jupiter Cycles**: The planet's alignment in different zodiac signs and its retrograde cycle shape its influence:
   - **Sagittarius and Pisces**: Jupiter rules Sagittarius and co-rules Pisces, where it thrives in expanding knowledge and spiritual pursuits.

- **Retrograde**: Jupiter retrograde (annually for four months) encourages inner exploration. Hemp can aid in reevaluating goals, reflecting on spiritual aspirations, and seeking personal truth.

Usage for Prosperity: Tips for Using Hemp to Attract Prosperity and Growth

To harness Jupiter's expansive energy through hemp, consider these practices and recipes:

1. **Abundance Rituals**:
   - **Hemp Candle Ritual**:
     - Create a ritual space with green hemp-infused candles, known for prosperity.
     - Light the candles and meditate on your intentions for growth, using hemp tinctures to deepen your focus.
   - **Prosperity Altar**:
     - Build an altar featuring hemp products, citrine crystals (symbolizing wealth), and gold coins.
     - Use this space for daily gratitude practices, visualizing prosperity flowing into your life.
2. **Nourishing Growth**:
   - **Hemp-Infused Smoothie**:
     - Blend 1 banana, 1 cup spinach, 1 tablespoon hemp protein powder, and 1 teaspoon spirulina with coconut water for a nutrient-packed smoothie.
     - Consume this regularly to promote physical vitality and creative energy, symbolizing Jupiter's potential for personal growth.
   - **Hemp Gardening**:
     - Plant hemp seeds when Jupiter is prominent to cultivate a physical representation of abundance.

- ■ Tend to the plants daily as a mindful practice, focusing on growth, gratitude, and prosperity.

3. **Spiritual Expansion:**
  - ° **Hemp Meditation Oils:**
    - ■ Mix hemp essential oil with sandalwood and frankincense oils.
    - ■ Use this blend in diffusers or apply it to your temples before meditation, expanding your spiritual awareness and fostering deep introspection.
  - ° **Hemp Journaling Practice:**
    - ■ Sip on hemp tea while journaling about personal goals and aspirations.
    - ■ Reflect on how hemp aligns with your intentions and ways to implement its growth-promoting qualities into your life.

Cosmic Hemp Pathways provides readers with a guide to harnessing Jupiter's expansive energies. By aligning Jupiter's benevolence with hemp's properties, individuals can nurture growth and prosperity, creating pathways for abundance and spiritual evolution.

Check out my Virtual dispensary for all your hemp needs: https://shift.store/sg1fan23477/retail

Chapter 9: Saturn and Hemp - Structure and Discipline

Saturnine Lessons: Enhancing Hemp's Benefits with Saturn's Structure and Discipline

Saturn, the planet associated with structure, responsibility, and discipline, governs life lessons that build strong foundations. Saturn's energies teach perseverance, patience, and mastery over time. In astrology, Saturn encourages us to uphold commitments, embrace structure, and take responsibility for our lives.

When paired with hemp's natural benefits, Saturnine influence can help us cultivate self-discipline, focus, and clarity. Hemp's calming and restorative properties complement Saturn's principles by easing the burdens of stress while maintaining steady, structured progress.

1. **Patience and Discipline**: Saturn's influence demands steady effort and dedication. Hemp's balancing effects can help us maintain patience, especially in times of frustration or delay.
2. **Structure and Stability**: Saturn promotes structure, which is essential for managing responsibilities. Hemp can encourage relaxation and clarity, helping us stick to schedules and keep organized.
3. **Wisdom and Mastery**: Saturn brings mastery through hard-won wisdom. Hemp's calming properties can enhance introspection and provide a level-headed perspective on past lessons.
4. **Saturnine Cycles**: Understanding the planet's cycles can aid in aligning its influence with hemp.
    - **Capricorn and Aquarius**: Saturn rules Capricorn and co-rules Aquarius, where its influence on diligence and innovation is strongest. Hemp can help balance the intense, goal-focused energy of Capricorn and the expansive, innovative mindset of Aquarius.
    - **Retrograde**: Saturn retrograde (annually for four and a half months) invites us to reevaluate our structures and

responsibilities. Hemp can provide clarity and resilience during this introspective period.

Structured Applications: Incorporating Hemp into Daily Routines for Self-Discipline

The following methods can be used to align Saturn's disciplined energy with hemp's benefits, fostering greater self-control and responsibility.

1. **Morning Ritual for Grounding:**
   - **Hemp Meditation Practice:**
     - Begin the morning with meditation. Light a hemp-infused candle and focus on your breathing.
     - Sip hemp tea or apply hemp essential oil to your temples for a clear, focused start to your day.
   - **Gratitude Journal:**
     - Write three things you're grateful for every morning while taking a hemp tincture to encourage clarity and positive intentions.
2. **Daily Organization and Planning:**
   - **Hemp Productivity Boost:**
     - Take micro-doses of hemp tincture or edibles before focusing on key tasks. Hemp's calming effects can help alleviate distractions and sharpen concentration.
   - **Task Lists and Breaks:**
     - Create structured to-do lists for the day, integrating short breaks for hemp teas or topical applications.
     - These breaks provide relaxation while reinforcing task completion and productivity.
3. **Evening Ritual for Reflection:**
   - **Introspection Practice:**
     - In the evening, write about your accomplishments and challenges from the day.

- ■ Take a hemp tincture or drink a hemp-infused herbal tea to encourage reflection and learn from the day's experiences.
- ∘ **Relaxing Bath Ritual:**
    - ■ Combine hemp essential oil with Epsom salts and lavender oil for a relaxing bath.
    - ■ This ritual can calm the mind and body, supporting Saturn's principles of recuperation and deliberate progress.

Cosmic Hemp Pathways guides readers to effectively use Saturn's structure and discipline in harmony with hemp's properties. By incorporating these practices into daily routines, individuals can foster self-discipline, wisdom, and sustainable progress, building a solid foundation for achieving their goals.

Chapter 10: Uranus, Neptune, and Pluto - Transformation and Beyond

Outer Planets: The Transformative Energies of Uranus, Neptune, and Pluto

The outer planets—Uranus, Neptune, and Pluto—symbolize deep, transformative energies that transcend the boundaries of daily existence. They govern the broader cycles of change, upheaval, and spiritual evolution in society and individuals. Their longer orbits mean that their influence manifests gradually but profoundly, shaping the subconscious and awakening transformative potentials.

1. **Uranus - Innovation and Awakening**: Uranus embodies the spirit of revolution, originality, and sudden change. Known for triggering breakthroughs and challenging conventions, Uranus aligns well with hemp's history of transformation and innovation. By leveraging Uranus' energies, hemp can facilitate new ways of thinking and help people explore uncharted territories in spirituality.

2. **Neptune - Mysticism and Imagination**: Neptune governs the realms of dreams, mysticism, and spirituality. Its influence dissolves barriers and blurs the line between reality and imagination. Hemp's calming and mildly psychoactive effects can deepen spiritual practices, enhance meditation, and foster a connection with the unseen.

3. **Pluto - Transformation and Rebirth**: Pluto represents transformation through the cycle of death and rebirth. It brings hidden truths to the surface, purging outdated patterns and promoting regeneration. Hemp's cleansing and restorative properties align with Pluto's potential to facilitate healing and spiritual rebirth.

Transformative Practices: Harnessing Hemp for Deep Spiritual Awakenings

By understanding how the outer planets influence our spiritual evolution, we can use hemp to foster transformative growth during their significant transits.

1. **Uranus Transits - Embracing Innovation:**
   - **Breaking Old Patterns:**
     - During Uranus transits, challenge old patterns by introducing new forms of meditation.
     - Use hemp tinctures to enhance meditation practice and break mental barriers, enabling unconventional insights.
   - **Revolutionizing Rituals:**
     - Integrate hemp into innovative rituals, such as sound baths or guided visualizations. Hemp's properties can foster creativity and support the adoption of new spiritual perspectives.
2. **Neptune Transits - Deepening Spiritual Connection:**
   - **Mystical Meditation:**
     - During Neptune transits, immerse yourself in mystical meditation to connect with your intuition.
     - Prepare a hemp-infused herbal tea with herbs like mugwort or chamomile to facilitate lucid dreaming and deep relaxation.
   - **Sacred Creativity:**
     - Harness Neptune's imaginative energy through creative activities like painting, journaling, or music.
     - Use hemp essential oils or tinctures to inspire creative flow and align your art with spiritual insight.
3. **Pluto Transits - Transformation and Rebirth:**
   - **Shadow Work Ritual:**
     - During Pluto transits, face inner shadows through introspective journaling or guided therapy.

- ■ Apply hemp-based balms to ease tension and create a safe space for emotional release.
  - ◦ **Rebirth Ceremonies:**
    - ■ After periods of deep shadow work, design a rebirth ceremony with hemp-infused candles and symbolic elements that represent your transformation.
    - ■ Use this space to meditate, acknowledging past challenges and welcoming your new self.

Cosmic Hemp Pathways guides readers through harnessing the outer planets' transformative energies with hemp's spiritual properties. By aligning Uranus, Neptune, and Pluto's significant transits with hemp-based practices, individuals can embrace personal awakenings, challenge norms, and emerge with newfound wisdom and purpose.

Check out my Virtual dispensary for all your hemp needs: https://shift.store/sg1fan23477/retail

Conclusion: Weaving Cosmic and Cannabis Synergies into Everyday Life

Recap: Unique Interactions Between Astrology and Hemp Explored

In *Cosmic Hemp Pathways*, we've journeyed through a fascinating blend of cosmic influences and the versatile properties of hemp, revealing how these two elements can enrich our lives. Here's a recap of the key insights and discoveries from each chapter:

1. **Introduction**: We unveiled the mystical alliance between hemp and astrology, establishing the purpose and foundational understanding necessary for exploring their interconnectedness.
2. **Chapter 1**: The historical journey of hemp highlighted its ancient and modern cultural significance, setting the stage for its holistic use today.
3. **Chapter 2**: An exploration of astrological basics revealed how celestial cycles and planetary influences directly relate to herbal healing practices.
4. **Chapter 3**: We linked hemp and the Sun, demonstrating how solar energy bolsters vitality and offers practical tips for optimal cultivation.
5. **Chapter 4**: The Moon's phases shape intuition and emotional healing, guiding the cultivation and use of hemp for spiritual practices and emotional balance.
6. **Chapter 5**: Mercury's influence on communication and cognition showed us how hemp can sharpen focus and support clearer thinking.
7. **Chapter 6**: Venus, ruling over harmony and relationships, illustrated how hemp can enhance beauty, love, and interpersonal connections.
8. **Chapter 7**: Mars revealed the energizing, assertive potential of hemp to boost physical activities and meet challenges.

9. **Chapter 8**: Jupiter's expansive energy and its alignment with hemp opened doors to spiritual growth and prosperity.
10. **Chapter 9**: Saturn's lessons emphasized structure and responsibility, outlining how hemp can support self-discipline and grounded progress.
11. **Chapter 10**: Uranus, Neptune, and Pluto introduced transformative energies that align hemp with personal awakenings and spiritual growth.

Integration: Embodying the Synergies for Holistic Well-being

Astrological insights and hemp's natural benefits provide potent tools for holistic well-being when incorporated into everyday practices. Here's how readers can integrate these principles:

1. **Daily Rituals**: Incorporate hemp tinctures, oils, and infusions into morning or evening meditation practices to align with the day's cosmic energies and set positive intentions.
2. **Physical and Mental Wellness**: Use hemp-based products strategically for physical health, such as soothing muscle balms after a workout, and mental clarity with herbal teas or micro-dosed tinctures.
3. **Cosmic Alignment**: Track significant planetary transits and lunar phases, aligning your intentions and practices with these cosmic influences. For instance, harness Mars transits to tackle challenging projects, or use lunar cycles to release emotional baggage.
4. **Creative Exploration**: Experiment with hemp-infused candles, art, and music to foster creativity and express your spiritual insights.

Future Exploration: Continuing the Cosmic Hemp Journey

Our exploration only scratches the surface of how hemp and astrology can work together for holistic health and spiritual fulfillment. As you continue your journey:

1. **Experiment and Reflect**: Keep a journal to document your experiences with different astrological practices involving hemp. Reflect on how these methods affect your well-being and spiritual growth.
2. **Research New Connections**: Stay curious and explore other astrological aspects that may resonate with your journey. For instance, investigate specific planetary alignments or star signs and their unique connections to hemp.
3. **Share and Inspire**: Engage with communities interested in holistic health and spirituality, sharing your insights and inspiring others to embrace the cosmic synergy.

In weaving cosmic and cannabis synergies into everyday life, you open a new realm of transformative potential that aligns body, mind, and spirit. May your path forward be enriched by these energies as you walk the cosmic hemp pathways to fulfillment.

Appendix A: Cultivating and Processing Hemp
Cultivation Tips: Practical Advice on Growing Hemp

1. **Understanding Hemp's Growth Requirements:**
   - **Climate and Soil**: Hemp thrives in well-drained soil with a pH of 6.0-7.5. It requires ample sunlight and warm temperatures for optimal growth.
   - **Watering**: Hemp needs sufficient water, particularly in the early stages of growth. However, avoid waterlogged soil.
2. **Selecting the Right Hemp Strain:**
   - **Purpose**: Choose strains based on your intended use. Fiber strains grow taller, while strains for seed production yield shorter, bushier plants.
   - **Legal Considerations**: Ensure the THC levels of the selected strain comply with local regulations.
3. **Astrological Timings for Planting and Harvesting:**
   - **New Moon**: Plant hemp seeds during the New Moon phase for increased growth energy.
   - **Full Moon**: Harvest during the Full Moon for optimum potency in medicinal applications.
   - **Solar Influence**: Plant hemp under favorable solar transits (e.g., Sun in Aries for vitality) to enhance germination and vigor.
   - **Mercury Retrograde**: Avoid planting or harvesting during Mercury retrograde to prevent delays and miscommunication.

4. **Planting and Growing Process:**
   - **Seed Germination:**
     - Soak seeds overnight in room-temperature water before sowing.
     - Plant seeds 1/2 inch deep in seed-starting trays or directly in the soil.
   - **Transplanting:**
     - Once seedlings are 4-6 inches tall, transplant them to their final location.
   - **Fertilization and Pest Control:**
     - Use organic fertilizers rich in nitrogen, phosphorus, and potassium.
     - Apply natural pest control measures like neem oil or companion planting (e.g., basil or marigold).
5. **Harvesting and Curing:**
   - **Timing:** Harvest when the leaves yellow, seeds are firm, and fiber reaches the desired quality.
   - **Curing:** Hang-dry hemp stalks or flowers for 2-4 weeks in a well-ventilated area to retain potency and texture.

Processing Techniques: Instructions for Various Uses

1. **Textiles:**
   - **Rett:** Bundle stalks and immerse them in water for 7-14 days to loosen fibers.
   - **Breaking and Scutching:**
     - Once dry, break stalks using a wooden breaker to separate fibers from the core.
     - Scutch the fibers against a wooden board to remove the remaining woody pieces.
   - **Hackling:** Draw the fibers through a series of combs to straighten and refine them.
2. **Seed Oil:**
   - **Pressing:**

- ■ Dry seeds thoroughly.
- ■ Use a mechanical press to extract oil, or cold-press for higher nutritional value.
  - ◦ **Filtering and Bottling**:
    - ■ Filter the extracted oil to remove impurities.
    - ■ Store in dark glass bottles away from sunlight.

3. **Medicinal Products**:
   - ◦ **Tinctures**:
     - ■ Decarboxylate dried hemp flowers by baking them at 240°F (115°C) for 30-40 minutes.
     - ■ Submerge the decarboxylated flowers in high-proof alcohol for 4-6 weeks, shaking occasionally.
     - ■ Strain the mixture and store the tincture in dark glass bottles.
   - ◦ **Topicals**:
     - ■ Infuse dried hemp flowers or hemp seed oil into a base of coconut or olive oil.
     - ■ Mix with beeswax to create a soothing balm for external application.

4. **Edibles**:
   - ◦ **Infused Oils and Butter**:
     - ■ Decarboxylate hemp flowers, then simmer them with oil or butter for 2-3 hours.
     - ■ Strain out plant material and use the infused product for cooking or baking.
   - ◦ **Hemp Milk**:
     - ■ Blend 1 cup of hemp seeds with 4 cups of water.
     - ■ Strain through a nut milk bag or fine-mesh sieve.
     - ■ Sweeten and flavor with vanilla extract or sweeteners as desired.

Cosmic Hemp Pathways provides a practical approach to cultivating and processing hemp, aligned with cosmic principles for optimal growth and usage. By understanding the unique timing and processing techniques, readers can create high-quality hemp products tailored to their personal needs and astrological preferences.

Appendix B: Astrology and Plant Care
Astrological Gardening: Using Astrological Principles for Plant Care
Astrological gardening uses the positions and movements of celestial bodies to inform planting, tending, and harvesting. Ancient wisdom and modern observations suggest that celestial influences can significantly impact plant growth. Here's how you can incorporate astrological principles into your gardening practice:

1. **Lunar Phases and Plant Growth:**
    ◦ **New Moon to Full Moon (Waxing Phase):**
        ▪ Ideal for planting and cultivating above-ground crops, including flowers and vegetables.
        ▪ The increasing lunar energy supports vigorous growth and robust development.
    ◦ **Full Moon to New Moon (Waning Phase):**
        ▪ Best for planting root crops and perennials, pruning, and transplanting.
        ▪ Waning lunar energy encourages strong root development.
2. **Zodiac Signs and Plant Types:**
    ◦ **Water Signs (Cancer, Scorpio, Pisces):**
        ▪ Best for leaf crops like lettuce, spinach, and herbs. The water element promotes moisture and nutrient uptake.
        ▪ Fertilizing and watering during these signs ensure healthy and hydrated plants.
    ◦ **Earth Signs (Taurus, Virgo, Capricorn):**
        ▪ Favorable for root crops like carrots, potatoes, and garlic due to the grounding energy of earth signs.
        ▪ Earth signs also support soil enrichment and composting.

- **Air Signs (Gemini, Libra, Aquarius):**
  - Ideal for flowers and pollinators due to their light and mobile energy.
  - These signs are suitable for cultivating herbs and plants that aid in intellectual pursuits.
- **Fire Signs (Aries, Leo, Sagittarius):**
  - Favorable for fruiting plants such as tomatoes, peppers, and squash.
  - Fire signs' warm energy also helps in drying herbs and spices.

3. **Planetary Influences on Plant Growth:**
   - **Sun:** The Sun's transit through zodiac signs influences the vitality and health of plants. Pay attention to seasonal transitions to adjust your gardening practices accordingly.
   - **Mercury:** During Mercury retrograde, avoid planting new crops or making major changes in the garden. Use this time for routine maintenance and addressing previous issues.
   - **Venus:** Venus enhances plant beauty and fragrance. It is an ideal time to plant flowers and ornamental herbs.
   - **Mars:** During Mars transits, prioritize pruning and weeding. Mars supports vigorous growth and resistance against pests.

Celestial Timing: Calendar of Astrological Events for Gardening Activities

Key Events:

1. **Equinoxes and Solstices:**
   - **Spring Equinox:** Start planting seeds and seedlings, as balanced light and warmth encourage growth.
   - **Summer Solstice:** Prune, harvest, and ensure crops are well-watered during the longest days of the year.
   - **Autumn Equinox:** Harvest late crops and plant cover crops to prepare for winter.

- **Winter Solstice**: Rest the garden, prepare soil, and plan next year's activities.

2. **Lunar Eclipses:**
   - Avoid planting or harvesting during lunar eclipses, as they bring heightened, unstable energy. Instead, focus on observation and strategic planning.

3. **Solar Eclipses:**
   - Solar eclipses can disrupt plant cycles, so use this time to reflect on previous successes and failures.

Astrological Calendar for Hemp:

1. **New Moon in Cancer** (Water Sign): Plant hemp seeds to encourage strong growth and moisture uptake.
2. **Full Moon in Capricorn** (Earth Sign): Harvest hemp for fiber or medicinal use, as potency will be at its peak.
3. **Sun in Aries** (Fire Sign): Prune and tend to young hemp plants, utilizing Aries' vigorous energy to strengthen their vitality.
4. **Mercury Direct** (Any Sign): Plan cultivation activities after Mercury retrograde for clear communication and efficient planning.
5. **Venus in Taurus** (Earth Sign): Ideal for nurturing plants for beauty and soothing effects. Incorporate fertilization and soil enrichment practices.

By combining astrological insights with practical plant care, readers can harmonize their hemp cultivation with cosmic rhythms. This alignment offers more intentional growth, optimized potency, and deeper spiritual connection through the seasons.

<u>Message from the Author:</u>

I hope you enjoyed this book, I love astrology and knew there was not a book such as this out on the shelf. I love metaphysical items as well. Please check out my other books:

-Life of Government Benefits

-My life of Hell

-My life with Hydrocephalus

-Red Sky

-World Domination:Woman's rule

-World Domination:Woman's Rule 2: The War

-Life and Banishment of Apophis: book 1

-The Kidney Friendly Diet

-The Ultimate Hemp Cookbook

-Creating a Dispensary(legally)

-Cleanliness throughout life: the importance of showering from childhood to adulthood.

-Strong Roots: The Risks of Overcoddling children

-Hemp Horoscopes: Cosmic Insights and Earthly Healing

- Celestial Hemp Navigating the Zodiac: Through the Green Cosmos

-Astrological Hemp: Aligning The Stars with Earth's Ancient Herb

-The Astrological Guide to Hemp: Stars, Signs, and Sacred Leaves

-Green Growth: Innovative Marketing Strategies for your Hemp Products and Dispensary

-Cosmic Cannabis

-Astrological Munchies

-Henry The Hemp

-Zodiacal Roots: The Astrological Soul Of Hemp

- **Green Constellations: Intersection of Hemp and Zodiac**

-Hemp in The Houses: An astrological Adventure Through The Cannabis Galaxy

-Galactic Ganja Guide

Heavenly Hemp

Zodiac Leaves

Doctor Who Astrology

Cannastrology

Stellar Satvias and Cosmic Indicas

<u>Celestial Cannabis: A Zodiac Journey</u>

AstroHerbology: The Sky and The Soil: Volume 1

AstroHerbology:Celestial Cannabis:Volume 2

Cosmic Cannabis Cultivation

The Starry Guide to Herbal Harmony: Volume 1

The Starry Guide to Herbal Harmony: Cannabis Universe: Volume 2

Yugioh Astrology: Astrological Guide to Deck, Duels and more

Nightmare Mansion: Echoes of The Abyss

Nightmare Mansion 2: Legacy of Shadows

Nightmare Mansion 3: Shadows of the Forgotten

Nightmare Mansion 4: Echoes of the Damned

The Life and Banishment of Apophis: Book 2

Nightmare Mansion: Halls of Despair

<u>Healing with Herb: Cannabis and Hydrocephalus</u>

<u>Planetary Pot: Aligning with Astrological Herbs: Volume 1</u>

Fast Track to Freedom: 30 Days to Financial Independence Using AI, Assets, and Agile Hustles

Check out my Virtual dispensary for all your hemp needs: https://shift.store/sg1fan23477/retail

If you want solar for your home go here: https://www.harborsolar.live/apophisenterprises/

<u>Instagrams:</u>
@apophis_enterprises,
@hempkingdom2024,
@apophisbookemporium,
@apophisfashion,
@apophisscardshop
Twitter: @apophisenterpr1, Tiktok:@apophisenterprise
Youtube: @sg1fan23477
Podcast:Apophis Chat Zone: https://open.spotify.com/show/5zXbrCLEV2xzCp8ybrfHsk?si=fb4d4fdbdce44dec
Newsletter: https://apophiss-newsletter-27c897.beehiiv.com/